Reading/Writing Companion

mheducation.com/prek-12

Send all inquiries to:
McGraw Hill
1325 Avenue of the Americas
New York, NY 10019

ISBN: 978-1-26-572845-8
MHID: 1-26-572845-3

Printed in the United States of America.

3 4 5 6 7 8 9 LMN 26 25 24 23 22

A

Welcome to WONDERS!

We are so excited about how much you will learn and grow this year! We're here to help you set goals for your learning.

You will build on what you already know and learn new things every day.

You will read a lot of fun stories and interesting texts on different topics.

You will write about the texts you read. You will also write texts of your own. You will do research as well.

You will explore new ideas by reading different texts.

Each week, we will set goals on the My Goals page. Here is an example:

I can read and understand realistic fiction.

I've never read realistic fiction. I'll shade the **first box**.

I want some more practice with realistic fiction, so I'll shade the first **two boxes**.

I can read and understand realistic fiction. I'll shade in **three boxes**.

I've read a lot of realistic fiction and I like to share what I know. I'll shade all **four boxes**.

As you read and write, you will learn skills and strategies to help you reach your goals.

You will think about your learning and sometimes fill in a bar to show your progress.

| Check In | 1 | 2 | 3 | 4 |

Here are some questions you can ask yourself.

- Did I understand the task?
- Was it easy?
- Was it hard?
- What made it hard?

It is okay if I need more practice. The most important thing is to do my best and keep learning!

If you need more support, you can choose what to do.

- Talk to a friend or teacher.
- Use an Anchor Chart.
- Choose a center activity.

At the end of each week, you will complete a fun task to show what you have learned.

Then you will return to your My Goals page and think about your learning.

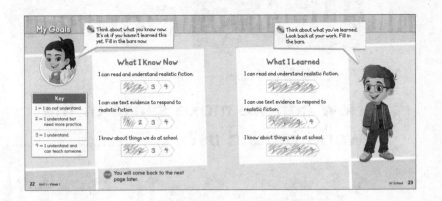

Unit 5 Figure It Out

The Big Idea

How can we make sense of the world around us? **8**

Week 1 • See It, Sort It

Week 2 • Up in the Sky

Week 3 • Great Inventions

Toru Yamanaka/AFP/Getty Images

Week 4 • Sounds All Around

5

Week 5 • Build It!

Extended Writing

How-To Text

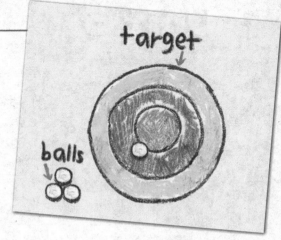

Connect and Reflect

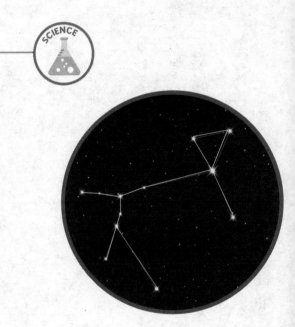

angelinast/Shutterstock

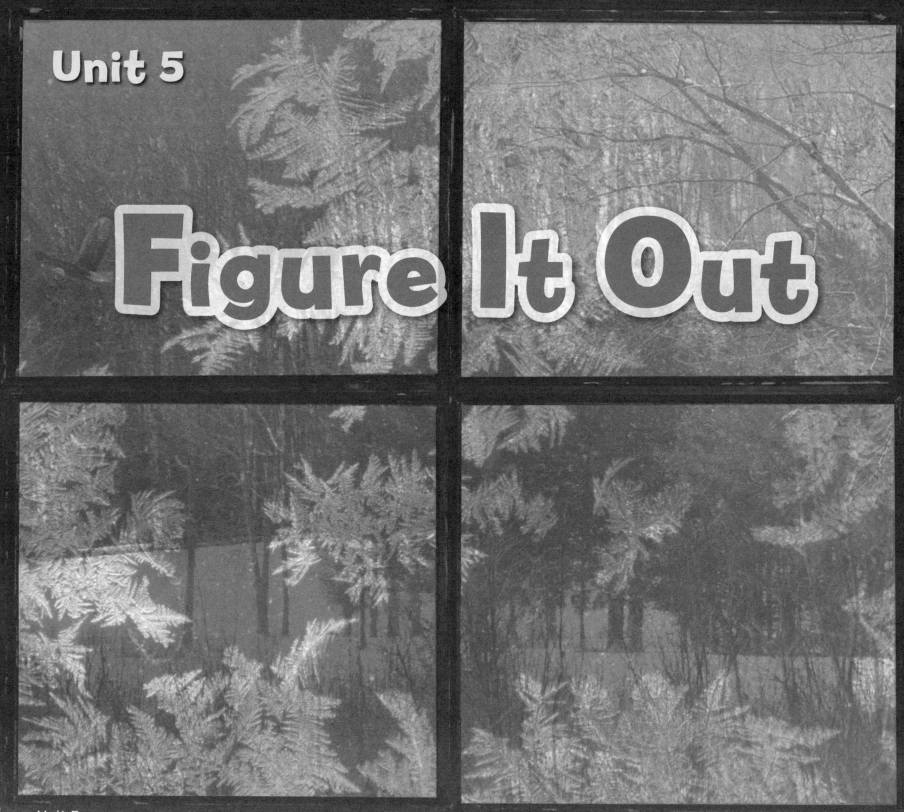

Unit 5

Figure It Out

Listen to and think about the poem "Jack Frost."

 Talk about what designs or shapes you see on the window in the photo.

The Big Idea

How can we make sense of the world around us?

Build Knowledge

? **Essential Question** How can we classify and categorize things?

Build Vocabulary

 Talk with your partner about ways we can sort things.

 Write words about sorting.

(color)

Ways to Sort

My Goals

 Think about what you know now. This may take time and effort! Fill in the bars.

What I Know Now

I can read and understand a fantasy story.

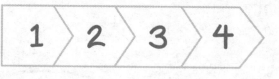
1 2 3 4

I can write an opinion about a fantasy story.

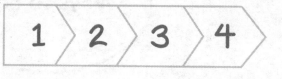
1 2 3 4

I know about ways we can classify and categorize things.

1 2 3 4

Key
1 = I do not understand.
2 = I understand but need more practice.
3 = I understand.
4 = I understand and can teach someone.

 You will come back to the next page later.

Think about what you've learned. What did you make progress with? Fill in the bars.

What I Learned

I can read and understand a fantasy story.

1 > 2 > 3 > 4

I can write an opinion about a fantasy story.

1 > 2 > 3 > 4

I know about ways we can classify and categorize things.

1 > 2 > 3 > 4

Shared Read

My Goal
I can read and understand a fantasy story.

🔍 **Find Text Evidence**

Read to find out how some farm animals sort hats.

Circle and read aloud the words with the *ar* sound as in *cart*.

Essential Question

? How can we classify and categorize things?

Clark's Farm

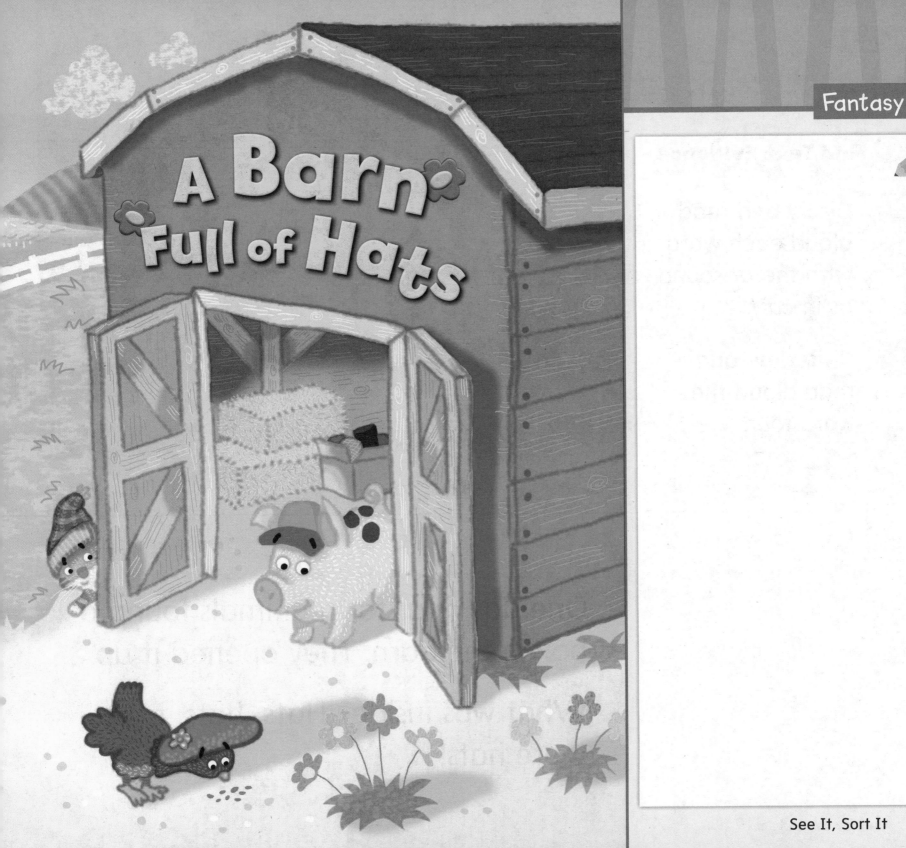

🔍 **Find Text Evidence**

○ **Circle** and read aloud each word with the *ar* sound as in *cart*.

Underline and read aloud the word *four*.

One day, four farm animals found a box in the barn. They opened it up.

What was inside? Hats, hats, and more hats!

"Look at all those hats! Who wants one?" asked Hen.

"I do!" cried Horse. "It's smart to wear a hat. A hat will keep the Sun out of my eyes."

Shared Read

 Underline and read aloud the words *round* and *put*.

Think about the story so far. Make a prediction about who will want the next hat.

Hen stuck her head in the box. She pulled out a flat, round hat. "Try this hat," Hen told Horse.

"No, that hat is too flat," said Horse.

"A flat hat makes a good nest!" clucked Hen. So she took the hat and she marched away.

Pig pushed his head in the box. He pulled out a bright red hat. "Put on this hat," Pig told Horse.

"No, that hat is too red," said Horse.

"A red hat looks fine!" grunted Pig. So he put on the hat and he marched away.

Find Text Evidence

 **Talk** about Horse. What have you learned about him so far?

Talk about the prediction you made about the next hat. Do you need to correct it?

Cat poked her head in the box. She pulled out a thick yarn hat. "Try this hat!" Cat told Horse.

"No, that hat is too thick," said Horse.

"Thick yarn is nice," said Cat. "I will take the **whole** hat apart, so I can play with the yarn." She dragged the hat away.

"So many hats, but none for me!" sighed Horse.

Find Text Evidence

Retell the events in order.

Just then, Farmer Clark came into the barn. His hat was large and floppy.

"If only I had that hat!" said Horse. "That hat will shade my eyes!"

Horse grabbed the hat in his teeth!

Farmer Clark laughed. He put the hat on Horse. It stayed on with no **trouble**. "It fits well," Farmer Clark said.

Horse trotted to the barnyard. Clip, clop! He held his head high. "Yes, this is the hat for me!" said Horse.

Write Sentences

Talk about the hats the animals chose.

Listen to these sentences about hats from the story.

> I would choose the bright red hat. Red is my favorite color. It is pretty!

Underline the longest sentence. Draw a box around the shortest sentence.

Circle the descriptive words.

Writing Traits

- **Vary sentence length** to make your sentences interesting.

- **Descriptive words** tell more about something or someone.

Talk about the hats from the story.

Write sentences about which hat you would choose. Vary your sentence lengths. Use descriptive words.

_____

_____

_____

_____

Underline the longest sentence. Draw a box around the shortest sentence.

Circle the descriptive words you used.

Check In 1 ⟩ 2 ⟩ 3 ⟩ 4 ⟩

Vocabulary

 Listen to the sentences and look at the photos.

 Talk about the words.

Write your own sentences using each word.

trouble

A goat can get into **trouble**.

_____

- -

_____

whole

The **whole** barn is painted red.

_____

- -

_____

Frank Naylor/Alamy Stock Photo; Steve Hamblin/Alamy Stock photo

Multiple Meanings

To figure out which meaning of a word is used, think about the other words in the story.

🔍 Find Text Evidence

I know that *cried* has more than one meaning. The words *"I do!"* tell me Horse is excited. I think *cried* in this story means "yelled out with excitement."

"I do!" cried Horse.

Your Turn

What words help you figure out the meaning of *bright* on page 19?

_____

- -

_____

A **fantasy** is a made-up story that could not really happen. It often has animal characters who act like people, and dialogue, or words that the characters say.

 Reread the dialogue in the story.

 Talk about what you learn about Horse from what he says.

Choose two characters from the story. Write what you learn about them from what they say.

Characters	What I Learn About Them

A **narrator** is who tells the story.

I. **The narrator can be a character in the story. This narrator uses the words** *I, me,* **and** *my.*

2. **The narrator can be a speaker outside the story. This narrator uses characters' names and words such as** *he, she, his,* **or** *her.*

 Reread "A Barn Full of Hats."

Talk about who is telling the story. Look for clues on pages 18 and 22.

Write the clues you found on pages 18 and 22. Use these clues to tell who the narrator is.

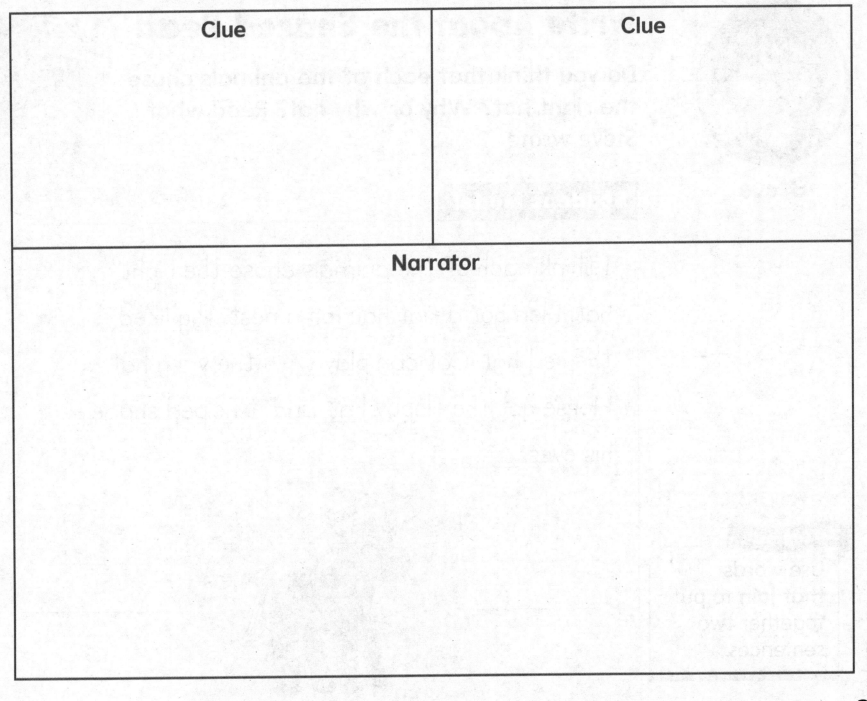

Clue	Clue

Narrator

Steve

Write About the Shared Read

Do you think that each of the animals chose the right hat? Why or why not? Read what Steve wrote.

Student Model

I think each of the animals chose the right hat. Hen got a flat hat for a nest. Pig liked the red hat. Cat can play with the yarn hat. Horse got the floppy hat, and it helped shade his eyes.

Grammar

Use **words that join** to put together two sentences.

Talk about details Steve used from the story. Underline the longest sentence.

 Circle a word that joins two sentences.

 Draw boxes around the descriptive words.

 Write what you notice about Steve's writing.

_____

- -

_____

- -

_____

- -

_____

A Lost Button
from Frog and Toad Are Friends
by Arnold Lobel

Retell the story using the illustrations and words from the story.

Write about the story. Use text evidence.

Why is the first button Frog finds not the right button?

_____
- -
_____
_____
- -
_____

Text Evidence

Page

What really happened to Toad's button?

_____
- -
_____
_____
- -
_____

Text Evidence

Page

Check In 1 2 3 4

Talk about what is happening in the story on page 144.

Write three things Frog says that show he is a good friend.

How does the author show that Frog is a good friend? Share your answer.

_____

- -

_____

- -

_____

Anchor Text

 Talk about how Toad acts when someone shows him a button on pages 148–149.

 Write three clues that show Toad's feelings.

How does the author show Toad's feelings?
Share your answer.

_____

- -

_____

_____

- -

_____

Talk about what Toad says on page 151.

Write clues from the text and illustration that tell you how Toad feels about Frog.

Clues from the Text	Clues from the Illustration

How does the author help you understand how Toad is a good friend? Share your answer.

_____

- -

_____

- -

_____

- -

Check In 1 > 2 > 3 > 4 >

Writing and Grammar

My Goal

I can write an opinion about a fantasy story.

Write About the Anchor Text

In *A Lost Button*, do you think Frog or Toad was the better friend? Why?

 Talk about the question.

 Write your answer below.

_____

_ _

_____

_ _

_____

_ _

_____

Remember:

☐ Vary sentence length.

☐ Use descriptive words.

☐ Use words that join correctly.

Check In 1 2 3 4

Sort It Out

Some things are alike. Some are different. We can sort things by looking at what is the same about them. We can sort them by their size, shape, and color.

Find the buttons in this picture. Let's sort them!

Read the title and look at the picture. Make a prediction about the text.

Underline the sentence that tells how to sort things.

Talk about how the picture helps you understand how to sort.

How many round buttons can you see? How many square buttons can you see? What other shapes do you see? Add up the number of red buttons. Are there more red or yellow buttons? Can you find buttons with four holes? How else could you sort these buttons?

 Talk about the picture and text. Do you need to change your prediction?

 Circle the words the author uses to describe the buttons.

 Talk about the author's purpose. What does the author want you to know?

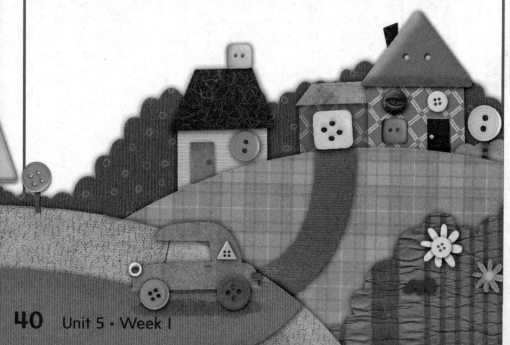

Quick Tip

You can use this sentence starter:

The author wants us to know …

Talk about the questions in the text. Where do you find the answers?

Write the answers to the last three questions the author asks on page 40.

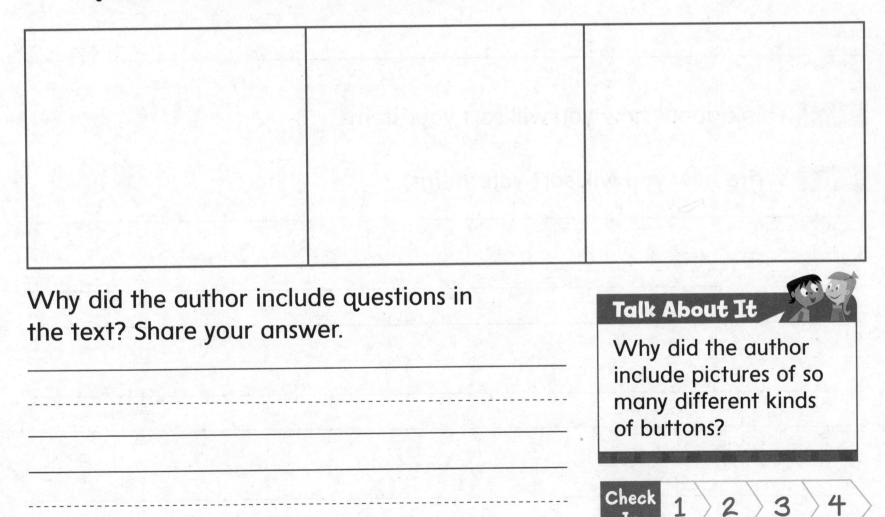

Why did the author include questions in the text? Share your answer.

_____

- -

_____

- -

_____

Talk About It

Why did the author include pictures of so many different kinds of buttons?

| Check In | 1 | 2 | 3 | 4 |

Sort a Collection

Step 1 **Choose** some items to collect and sort.
Write what you will collect.

_____

- -

_____

_____

Step 2 **Think** about how you will sort your items.

Step 3 **Write** how you will sort your items.

_____

- -

_____

_____

- -

_____

_____

- -

_____

Step 4 Collect your items. Then sort and tally your items.

Type	Number

Step 5 Write what you learned.

_____

- -

_____

- -

_____

- -

_____

_____

_____

- -

_____

Step 6 Choose how to present your work.

Check In 1 ⟩ 2 ⟩ 3 ⟩ 4 ⟩

Talk about how the poet sorts the coins in the poem.

 Compare how the items in the poem and the buttons in "Sort It Out" can be sorted.

In My Bank

I have a little bank.
It's filled right to the top.
I need to sort these coins
to see how much I've got.
I see quarters, dimes, and pennies
now sorted into piles.
Wow, I have so many.
You can see my smile for miles!

Check In   1 2 3 4

Write a Nonfiction Text

1 **Look** at your Build Knowledge pages in your reader's notebook. Talk with your partner about how we can classify and categorize things.

2 **Write** about three ways we can sort things. Use text evidence. Use two vocabulary words from the Word Bank.

3 **Draw** a picture to go with your nonfiction text.

Think about what you learned this week. Fill in the bars on page 13.

Build Knowledge

? Essential Question **What can you see in the sky?**

Build Vocabulary

 Talk with your partner about things we can see in the sky.

 Write words about the sky.

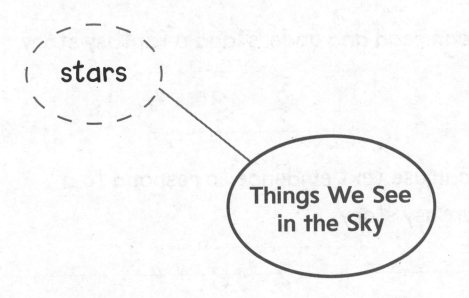

(stars)

Things We See in the Sky

My Goals

 Think about what you know now. We'll learn new things all week. Fill in the bars.

What I Know Now

I can read and understand a fantasy story.

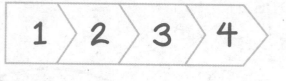

I can use text evidence to respond to a fantasy story.

I know about things we can see in the sky.

Key
1 = I do not understand.
2 = I understand but need more practice.
3 = I understand.
4 = I understand and can teach someone.

 You will come back to the next page later.

Think about what you've learned.
Look back at your work. Fill in
the bars.

What I Learned

I can read and understand a fantasy story.

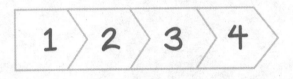

I can use text evidence to respond to a
fantasy story.

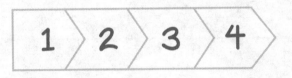

I know about things we can see in the sky.

Shared Read

My Goal

I can read and understand a fantasy story.

 Find Text Evidence

Read to find out how a bird named Fern learns about clouds.

Circle and read aloud the word spelled with *ir* as in *skirt*.

Essential Question

? What can you see in the sky?

A Bird Named Fern

Shared Read

🔍 **Find Text Evidence**

✏️ ⭕ **Circle** and read aloud the word spelled with *or* as in *worm*.

👫 **Make** a prediction about what Fern will do next.

Little Fern was always full of questions! She wanted to know about everything in the world.

One day, Fern saw something up in the sky.

"What is that big white boat doing in the sky?" she asked herself. "I want to find out."

Read

Shared Read

 Find Text Evidence

Underline and read aloud the words *great* and *climb*.

Talk about the prediction you made about Fern. Correct it if you need to.

"It would be great to ride on that big white boat," Fern said. So she **stretched** her wings and took off.

Fern's wings helped her climb up, up, up.

But when she got close to the boat, she was surprised. The boat looked like a fluffy bed!

Shared Read

 Underline and read aloud the words *through* and *another*.

Talk about why Fern fell through the beds.

Fern was sleepy and wanted to rest. So she **leaped** on the bed. But she fell right through it!

"I see another bed," said Fern.
"I will try to land on that one."

But the same thing happened again!

"I'd better go home," cried Fern.
"Maybe Mom and Dad can
explain this."

 **Find Text Evidence**

Retell the story using the illustrations and words to help you.

So Fern began to fly home. As she did, the beds turned dark gray. Then it started to rain. Poor Fern was soaked when she got home.

"Where were you?" asked Mom and Dad.

Fern told them all about her trip.

"First we will dry you off," said Mom.

"Then we will teach you about clouds," added Dad.

And that is what they did!

Write Sentences

 Talk about what Fern saw in the clouds.

 Listen to these sentences about things we can see in the sky.

> Tom and I spotted the North Star last night! It twinkled so bright. We gasped when we saw it!

 Underline the strong verbs.

Circle the main idea.

Writing Traits

- **Strong verbs** help readers know how something or someone moves.

- Make sure your writing **focuses on one idea.**

Talk about a time you saw something in the sky.

 Write sentences about a time you saw something in the sky. Use strong verbs. Focus on one idea.

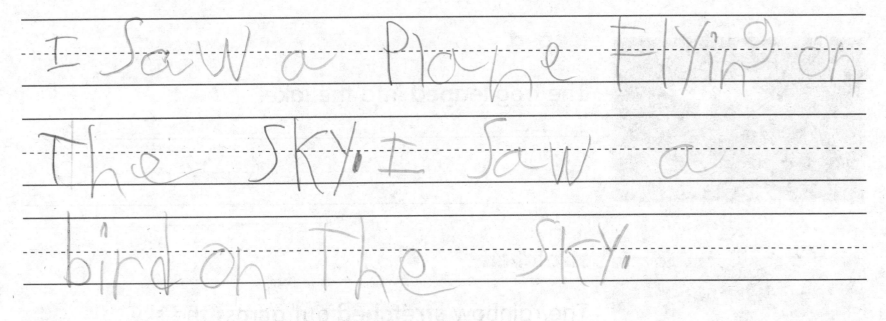

I saw a Plane Flying on The Sky. I saw a bird on The Sky.

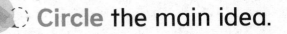 **Underline** the strong verbs you used.

Circle the main idea.

Vocabulary

 Listen to the sentences and look at the photos.

 Talk about the words.

 Write your own sentences using each word.

leaped

The frog **leaped** into the lake.

_____

- -

_____

stretched

The rainbow **stretched** out across the sky.

_____

- -

_____

Michael Leach/Oxford Scientific/Getty Images; Dave G Kelly/Moment Select/Getty Images

Think about small differences in meaning between words to better understand what you read.

Find Text Evidence

I know *great* and *good* have similar meanings, but *great* means "wonderful." I can tell that Fern thinks riding the boat would be more than just good!

> "It would be great to ride on that big white boat," Fern said.

Your Turn

Think about the word *soaked* on page 58. What word do you know with just a small difference in meaning?

_____

- -

_____

Check In   1 ⟩ 2 ⟩ 3 ⟩ 4 ⟩

Remember, a **fantasy** is a story with made-up characters and events that could not happen in real life.

Reread and think about the characters.

Talk about what makes this a fantasy story. Think about the characters and events.

Write how you know the story is a fantasy.

Characters and Events	Why It Could Not Happen in Real Life

In stories, sometimes one event can cause another event to happen. Remember, a cause is what makes something happen in a story. An effect is the event that happens.

 Reread "A Bird Named Fern."

 Talk about what happens on pages 54-55 and why it happens.

Write about the story by giving details about causes and effects.

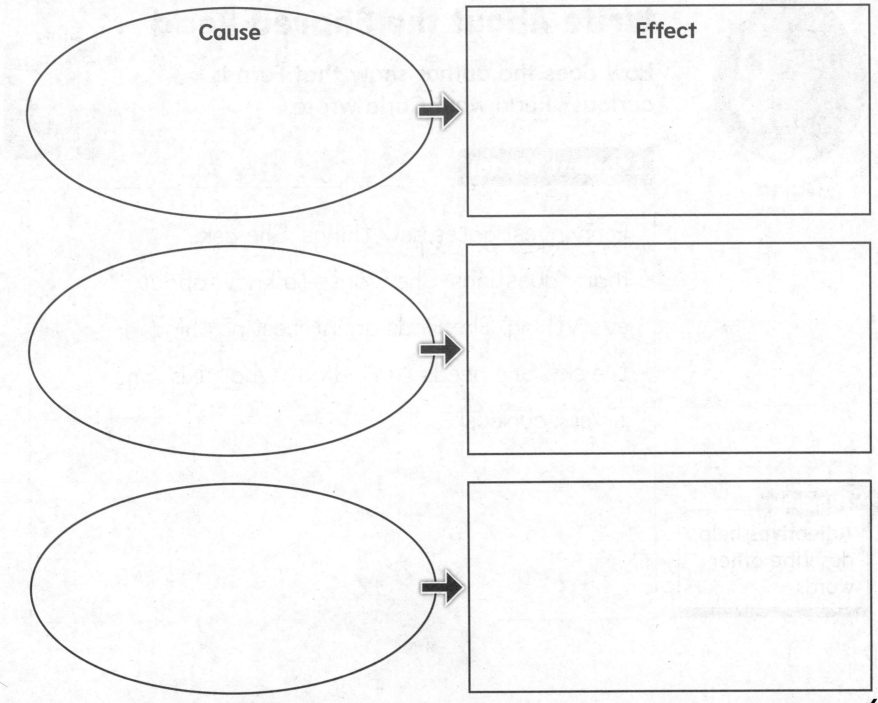

Cause

Effect

Carla

Write About the Shared Read

How does the author show that Fern is curious? Read what Carla wrote.

Student Model

Fern investigates new things. She asks many questions. She wants to know about everything. She finds an interesting thing in the sky. She needs to find out what it is. She is very curious!

Steve Debenport/E+/Getty Images

Grammar

Adjectives help describe other words.

Talk about details Carla used from the story. Draw a box around the strong verb in the first sentence.

Circle the adjective in the fourth sentence.

Underline the main idea.

Write what you notice about Carla's writing.

Quick Tip

You can talk about Carla's writing using these sentence starters:

I noticed . . .
Carla used . . .

She PuT pirieT all SenTenS

👧👦 **Retell** the story using the illustrations and words from the story.

🔷 **Write** about the story.

Why does Kitten keep trying to get the Moon?

_____
- - - - - - - - - - - - - - - - - -
_____
- - - - - - - - - - - - - - - - - -
_____

Text Evidence

🔍

Page

What finally makes Kitten "Lucky Kitten" instead of "Poor Kitten"?

_____
- - - - - - - - - - - - - - - - - -
_____
- - - - - - - - - - - - - - - - - -
_____

Text Evidence

🔍

Pages

Check In 1 2 3 4

Talk about what Kitten tries to do on pages 166 and 170.

 Write about what Kitten tries to do to the Moon each time. Talk about this pattern.

First, Kitten tries . . .	Then, Kitten tries . . .

What is the author's purpose for using this pattern? Share your answer.

_____

_____

_____

_____

_____

 Talk about the sentence that the author repeats on pages 168–169 and 172–173.

Write the sentence. Then write what the sentence helps you visualize.

Repeated Sentence	What I Visualize

Why does the author repeat the sentence?
Share your answer.

_____

- -

_____

- -

_____

Talk about what Kitten sees on pages 180–181.

Write clues that show what Kitten thinks.

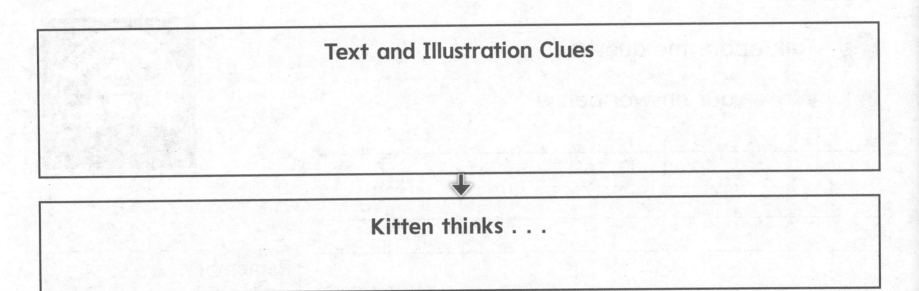

Text and Illustration Clues

Kitten thinks . . .

How do the text and illustration help you understand what is happening in the story? Share your ideas.

_____

_____

_____

Check In 1 2 3 4

Writing and Grammar

Write About the Anchor Text

My Goal I can use text evidence to respond to a fantasy story.

How does the author show that Kitten is curious?

 Talk about the question.

 Write your answer below.

_____

- -

_____

_____

- -

_____

_____

- -

_____

Remember:

☐ Use strong verbs.

☐ Focus on one idea.

☐ Use adjectives in your writing.

Check In 1 2 3 4

The Moon

In the past, some people thought that the Moon was made of cheese. Some saw the face of a man in the Moon.

Then telescopes helped us see the Moon better. The telescopes showed hills and flat places. They showed craters, or big holes, too.

We can see the Moon better with a telescope.

Steve Cole/Photographer's Choice/Getty Images; (inset) somchaisom/iStock/360/Getty Images

Then, in 1961, astronauts went into space. In 1969, other astronauts walked on the Moon! They got a real close-up look.

Nothing grows on the Moon. It is very rocky. Astronauts brought back Moon rocks for us to see.

Maybe one day you will go to the Moon, too!

 Circle two details that describe the Moon.

 Talk about your prediction. Did the photo and caption change it? How?

Talk about how the author feels about astronauts walking on the Moon.

Astronauts went into space and landed on the Moon.

NASA Headquarters - Greatest Images of NASA (NASA-HQ-GRIN)

Quick Tip

Use sentence starters to talk about the caption:

The author feels . . .

The author says . . .

Talk about what people used to think the Moon was made of.

 Write about what people thought about the Moon. Then write what they learned.

What People Thought About the Moon	Facts People Learned About the Moon

Why does the author tell what people once thought about the Moon? Share your answer.

_____

_____

_____

_____

Talk About It

Compare what we know about the Moon today with what we knew about it in the past.

Check In 1 2 3 4

The Sun Helps Us

Step 1 Think about how the Sun helps us.

Step 2 Write questions about the Sun.

_____

- -

_____

_____

- -

_____

_____

- -

_____

Step 3 Find books or websites to find the information you need.

Step 4 **Write** the answers to your questions.

_____
- -
_____
_____
- -
_____

Step 5 **Draw** and label what you learned about our Sun and how it helps us.

Step 6 **Choose** how to present your work.

Check In 1 > 2 > 3 > 4 >

Talk about what you see in this photo. Use complete sentences.

Compare how the sky in the photo is similar to and different from the sky in "The Moon."

Quick Tip

Use sentence starters to describe the photo.

The sky in the photo is . . .
I can see . . .

This person paraglides in the open sky above the mountains.

Mario Eder/Moment/Getty Images

Check In 1 2 3 4

Create a Sky Collage

1 **Look** at your Build Knowledge pages in your reader's notebook. Talk with your partner about what we can see in the sky.

2 **Create** a sky collage. Think about the texts you read. Make one side of the collage show things in the daytime sky. Make the other side show things in the nighttime sky. Include things you read about.

3 **Write** about your collage. Use two vocabulary words from the Word Bank.

Think about what you learned this week. Fill in the bars on page 49.

Build Knowledge

Essential Question What inventions do you know about?

Build Vocabulary

 Talk with your partner about inventions you know.

 Write words about inventions.

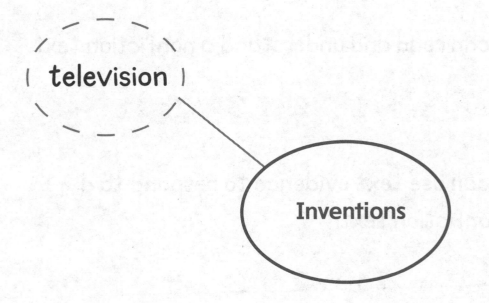

television

Inventions

My Goals

Think about what you know now. What do you need to practice more? Fill in the bars.

What I Know Now

I can read and understand a nonfiction text.

1 2 3 4

I can use text evidence to respond to a nonfiction text.

1 2 3 4

I know about different inventions.

1 2 3 4

Key

1 = I do not understand.

2 = I understand but need more practice.

3 = I understand.

4 = I understand and can teach someone.

 You will come back to the next page later.

Think about what you've learned. How did you do? Fill in the bars.

What I Learned

I can read and understand a nonfiction text.

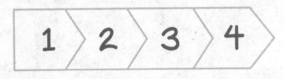
1 > 2 > 3 > 4

I can use text evidence to respond to a nonfiction text.

1 > 2 > 3 > 4

I know about different inventions.

1 > 2 > 3 > 4

My Goal

I can read and understand a nonfiction text.

🔍 **Find Text Evidence**

Read to find out about a robot inventor.

Look at the photo. What do you notice about the robots?

Essential Question

? What inventions do you know about?

The Story of a Robot Inventor

Shared Read

 Find Text Evidence

Circle and read aloud the words with the *or* sound as in *for*.

Ask a question about the text. Read to find the answer to your question. Then tell the answer using full sentences.

Big Ideas

Meet Tomotaka Takahashi. He invents **unusual** robots. How did he get started?

Mr. Takahashi was born in Japan in 1975. As a child, he played with blocks. He used his imagination to make all sorts of forms and shapes.

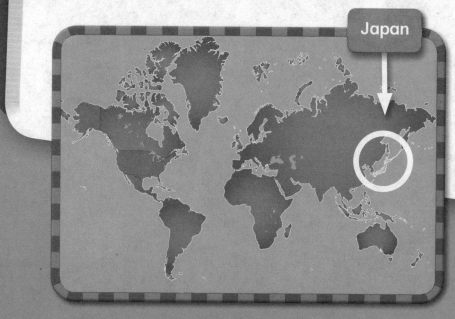

Japan

Later, he read comic books about robots. One of the robots looked like a real child. Takahashi wanted to make robots just like it.

Find Text Evidence

Circle and read aloud the word spelled with *ore* as in *chore*.

Underline and read aloud the words *began*, *learn*, *right*, and *better*.

Finding Out About Robots

In 1999, Takahashi began to study robots. He took classes to learn how they move. The robots bent their legs when they walked. It did not look right to Takahashi. People did not walk that way.

Then Takahashi had an **idea**. He made a better robot. It did not bend its legs when it walked. It moved more like a person.

Shared Read

Franck Robichon/EPA/Newscom

Find Text Evidence

Use clues from the text to figure out which robot is the strongest. Talk about your answer.

Talk about how you can tell Takahashi is good with robots.

Making Better Robots

In 2003, Takahashi started his own company. He made many robots. A short robot climbed up a cliff with a rope. A bigger robot lifted a car with its arms. Another robot rode a bike for 24 hours.

Takahashi began to put his robots in contests. He made three robots for a sports race in Hawaii in 2011. The first robot had to swim. The second robot had to ride a bike. The third robot had to run. The robots had to do these tasks for a week!

Toru Yamanaka/AFP/Getty Images

Shared Read

🔍 **Find Text Evidence**

Ask a question if you do not understand something. Reread to find the answers.

Retell the text so it makes sense.

For the race, there were many problems to solve. Takahashi made the swimming robot waterproof. He gave it arms like fins to help it swim faster. Another robot was able to ride its bike for 100 miles without breaking. The third robot ran for 26 miles!

What will Takahashi invent next? Will his robots fly and soar? Will they be his finest? We can only guess. We must wait and see.

Tomotaka Takahashi is sure of one thing. His robots will do more and more!

Writing Practice

Write Sentences

 Talk about Tomotaka Takahashi's inventions.

Listen to these sentences about robots.

> If I had a robot, it would do a lot of tricks! First, it would run. Then, it would hop. Last, it would flip.

 Underline the words that tell you the order of events.

Circle the first complete sentence.

Writing Traits

- Use the words *first, next,* and *last* to tell the order of events.

- You can vary sentence lengths to make your writing interesting.

Talk about a robot you would like to have.

 Write sentences about what your robot can do. Use words to tell the order of events. Write in complete sentences.

MY Robot can Play and I
WanT mY robot To Look
like me!

 Underline the words that tell the order of events.

Circle the first complete sentence.

Vocabulary

 Listen to the sentences and look at the photos.

 Talk about the words.

Write your own sentences using each word.

idea

New bulbs are a good **idea**!

_____

- - - - - - - - - - - - - - - - -

_____

unusual

This new bike is **unusual**.

_____

- - - - - - - - - - - - - - - - -

_____

If a word is new to you, look for parts you know to figure out the meaning.

Find Text Evidence

I'm not sure what *unusual* means, but I know that *usual* means "common." The prefix *un-* means "not." I think *unusual* means "not common."

He invents un|usual robots.

Your Turn

Write the parts in *unlike*. What does it mean?

_____

- -

_____

- -

_____

Check In 1 > 2 > 3 > 4 >

Toru Yamanaka/AFP/Getty Images

A **biography** is a story about a real person's life.
It is written by another person.

 Reread to find out what makes this text
a biography.

 Talk about how you know it is a biography.

Write the clues from the text that show
this is a biography.

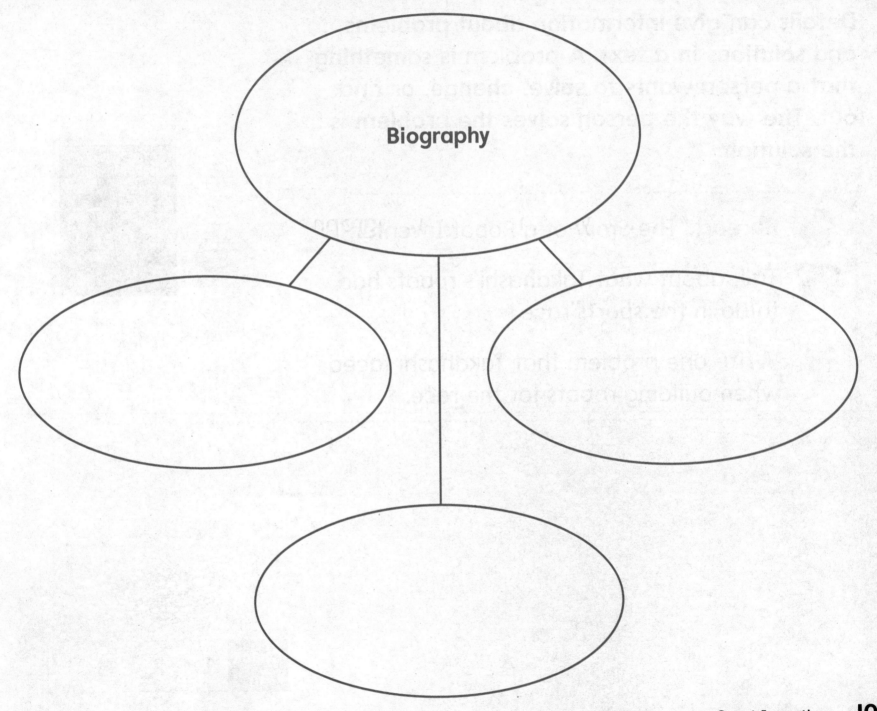

Biography

Details can give information about problems and solutions in a text. A **problem** is something that a person wants to solve, change, or find out. The way the person solves the problem is the **solution**.

The Story of a
Robot Inventor

 Reread "The Story of a Robot Inventor."

 Talk about what Takahashi's robots had to do in the sports race.

Write one problem that Takahashi faced when building robots for the race.

Check In 1 > 2 > 3 > 4

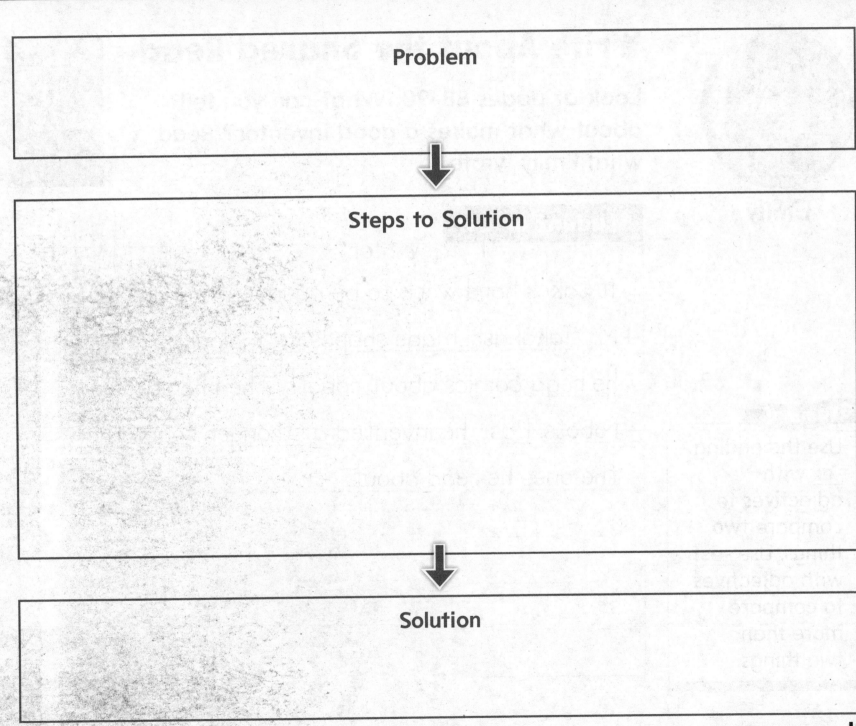

Problem

Steps to Solution

Solution

Writing and Grammar

Emily

Write About the Shared Read

Look at pages 88–90. What can you tell about what makes a good inventor? Read what Emily wrote.

The Story of a Robot Inventor

Student Model

It takes hard work to be an inventor. First, Mr. Takahashi made shapes with blocks. Next, he read comics about robots. Then he studied robots. Last, he invented a stronger robot than the ones he read about.

Grammar

Use the ending **-er** with adjectives to compare two things. Use **-est** with adjectives to compare more than two things.

Talk about details Emily used from the text. Underline the words that tell the order of events.

 Circle the adjective that compares.

 Draw a box around the last complete sentence.

Write what you notice about Emily's writing.

Quick Tip

You can use these sentence starters:

Emily used . . .
I noticed . . .

_____

- -

_____

- -

_____

- -

_____

- -

_____

- -

_____

Thomas Edison, Inventor

👫 **Retell** the text using the photos and words from the text.

✏️ **Write** about the text.

What made Thomas Edison want to do experiments?

_____

- -

_____

- -

_____

🔍 **Text Evidence**

Page

What was important to Tom as a teenager?

_____

- -

_____

- -

_____

🔍 **Text Evidence**

Page

Check In 1 ⟩ 2 ⟩ 3 ⟩ 4 ⟩

Talk about what you learn about young Tom on pages 204–207.

Write what young Tom wanted to know. What did he do to find out about it?

Tom wanted to know . . .	Tom experimented by . . .

Why does the author include stories about Tom Edison when he was young? Share your ideas.

_____

- -

_____

_____

- -

_____

 Talk about what you learn about Tom on pages 210–214.

Write what Tom did and why.

What Tom Edison Did	Why He Did It

Why does the author include stories about Thomas Edison as he got older? Share your ideas.

_____

- -

_____

- -

_____

Talk about page 214. How did people send messages before there were telephones?

 Write the steps Tom took that led him to invent new ways to use the telegraph.

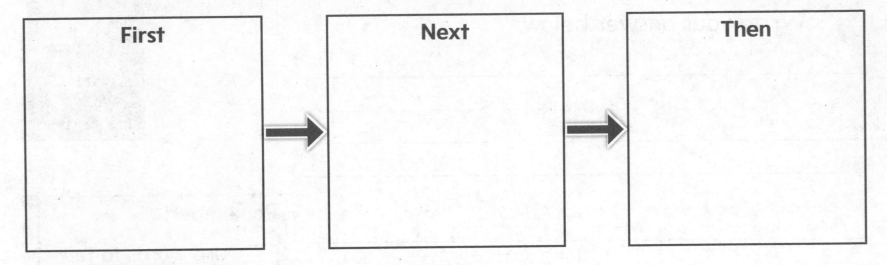

First

Next

Then

How does the author show that Tom kept trying new things? Share your answer.

_____

- -

_____

- -

Check In 1 ⟩ 2 ⟩ 3 ⟩ 4 ⟩

Writing and Grammar

Write About the Anchor Text

What made Thomas Edison a good inventor?

 Talk about the question.

Write your answer below.

_____

- -

_____

_____

- -

_____

_____

- -

_____

Remember:

☐ Use words to tell the order of events.

☐ Use complete sentences.

☐ Use adjectives that compare correctly.

Check In 〉 1 〉 2 〉 3 〉 4 〉

Talk about the words the author repeats.

Write the repeated words. What do they tell you about windshield wipers?

Repeated Words	What They Tell About Windshield Wipers

Why does the author repeat the words?
Share your ideas.

_____

_____

_____

_____

Talk about what scissors look like.

Write what the author writes at the start and end of the poem to tell what *X* means.

Start	End

Why does the author start and end the poem with the letter *X*? Share your ideas.

_____

- -

_____

_____

- -

_____

Quick Tip

Think about what you know about scissors.

Scissors look like . . .

When you open scissors, they . . .

Read aloud with a partner the words in the poems that begin with the same sounds.

Write the words with the same beginning sounds in each poem.

Windshield Wipers	Scissors

How do the words make the poem feel?

_____

- - - - - - - - - - - - - - - - - - - -

_____

- - - - - - - - - - - - - - - - - - - -

_____

Write About It

Write your own poem about a great invention. Use repeating words or words that begin with the same sounds.

Check In | 1 | 2 | 3 | 4

Find Out About an Inventor

Step 1 **Choose** an inventor from this week to learn more about.

_____
- -
_____

Step 2 **Decide** what else you want to know about your inventor. Write your questions.

_____
- -
_____
_____
- -
_____
- -
_____

Step 3 **Find** the information you need in books or online. Read for answers to your questions.

Step 4 **Write** notes about your inventor. Use a dictionary to look up words to tell about your inventor.

_____

- -

_____

- -

_____

- -

_____

- -

_____

Step 5 **Choose** how to present your findings. You may want to pretend to be your inventor and tell the class about yourself.

Check In 1 > 2 > 3 > 4 >

Talk about why this invention is a good idea.

 Compare the invention in the photo to the inventions Thomas Edison came up with to solve problems.

Quick Tip

Explain about the invention using these sentence starters:

Some people need . . .

The invention helps . . .

This child's hand can move and hold things, just like a real hand.

Mirrorpix/Newscom

Check In 1 2 3 4

Show Your Knowledge

I know about different inventions.

Write a Nonfiction Text

1 **Look** at your Build Knowledge pages in your reader's notebook. What did you learn about inventions?

2 **Choose** three texts you have read about inventions this week. Write about how inventions have made life easier in each of these texts. Use two vocabulary words from the Word Bank.

3 **Draw** a picture to go with your writing.

Think about what you learned this week. Fill in the bars on page 85.

Build Knowledge

Build Vocabulary

 Talk with your partner about how we can make different sounds.

 Write words about sounds.

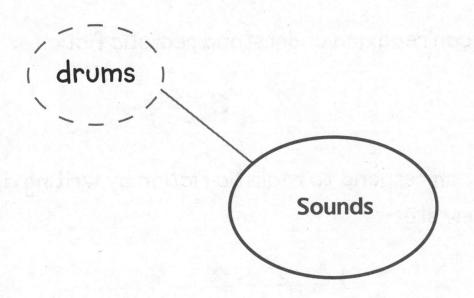

drums

Sounds

My Goals

Think about what you know now. What do you want to work on more? Fill in the bars.

What I Know Now

I can read and understand realistic fiction.

| 1 | 2 | 3 | 4 |

I can respond to realistic fiction by writing a new story.

| 1 | 2 | 3 | 4 |

I know about sounds and how they are made.

| 1 | 2 | 3 | 4 |

Key

1 = I do not understand.

2 = I understand but need more practice.

3 = I understand.

4 = I understand and can teach someone.

 STOP You will come back to the next page later.

 Think about what you've learned. What did you get better at? Fill in the bars.

What I Learned

I can read and understand realistic fiction.

1 > 2 > 3 > 4

I can respond to realistic fiction by writing a new story.

1 > 2 > 3 > 4

I know about sounds and how they are made.

1 > 2 > 3 > 4

My Goal I can read and understand realistic fiction.

 Find Text Evidence

 Think about the title and illustration. Ask a question about the story. Read on to find the answer.

Circle each word with the sound you hear in the middle of *found* and *down*.

Essential Question

? What sounds can you hear? How are they made?

Now, What's That Sound?

Underline and read aloud the words *early* and *thought*.

Ask a question about the sounds the kids hear. Read to find the answer.

Tap-tap-tap. Rat-a-tat-tat.

"What's that sound?" asked Gilbert. "It started early this morning. I thought it might stop, but it hasn't!"

"Let's check out the garage," said Marta. "I think Dad is making the sound."

Zing
Zing
Zing

Dad was in the garage cutting a board with his saw.

Zing, zing, zing.

"This is not the sound," said Gilbert. "This sound is smoother."

Find Text Evidence

Circle and read aloud each word on page 126 with the sound you hear in the middle of *found*.

Compare the sound Gramps is making to the sound the children are looking for.

"Let's find Gramps," said Marta. "He might be making the sound."

They quickly ran to the back of the house to find Gramps.

Gramps was sweeping the deck with a broom.

Swish, swish, swish.

"No, this is not the sound," said Gilbert. "This sound is much softer."

Find Text Evidence

Underline and read aloud the word *instead*.

Talk about why Marta says "This is hopeless!"

"Let's find Ana instead," said Marta. "Maybe she's making the sound."

They found Ana in the driveway. Ana was bouncing a ball.

Bam. . . bam . . . bam.

"No, this is not the sound," said Gilbert. "This sound is slower."

"This is hopeless!" sighed Marta.

Ask any other questions you have. Reread to find the answers.

 Retell the story so it makes sense.

Tap-tap-tap. Rat-a-tat-tat.

"There it is again," said Gilbert. He looked up at the tallest tree. **Suddenly**, he shouted. "Oh, wow! It's a bird!"

"Look at the color on its head," cried Marta. "It's red, like a red crown."

The bird **scrambled** up and down the tree.

Tap-tap-tap. Rat-a-tat-tat.

Find Text Evidence

Tap-tap-tap!
Rat-a-tat-tat!

"It's a woodpecker pecking for bugs," said Gilbert.

"Yes," said Marta. "And nothing else sounds like it!"

Tap-tap-tap! Rat-a-tat-tat!

Writing Practice

Write Sentences

 Talk about the sounds Gilbert and Marta hear in the story.

 Listen to these sentences about a sound at school.

Now, What's That Sound?

Nat and I hear birds tweeting in our school. Where are they? We look in the music room. It's Pam practicing the flute!

 Underline the beginning of each sentence.

 Talk about the beginning, middle, and end.

Writing Traits

- Begin each sentence differently so they don't all sound the same.

- The **beginning, middle,** and **end** of a story each tell events at different times in a story.

Talk about sounds you hear at home.

Write sentences about sounds you hear at home. Begin each sentence differently. Make sure you include a beginning, middle, and end.

_____

- -

_____

- -

_____

- -

_____

 Underline the beginning of each sentence.

 Talk about the beginning, middle, and end.

Vocabulary

 Listen to the sentences and look at the photos.

 Talk about the words.

 Write your own sentences using each word.

scrambled

Goats **scrambled** up the rocks.

_____

- -

_____

suddenly

The sky **suddenly** lit up brightly!

_____

- -

_____

If you don't know what a word means, look for word parts to help you figure out the meaning.

Find Text Evidence

I see the suffix *-less* at the end of the word *hopeless*. I can use the meaning of *-less* to figure out that *hopeless* means "without hope."

"This is hope(less)!" sighed Marta.

Your Turn

Use what you know about the meaning of the suffix *-ly* to figure out the meaning of the word *quickly* on page 126.

_____

- -

_____

Check In 1 > 2 > 3 > 4 >

Realistic fiction is a made-up story that has characters, a setting, and events that can happen in real life. It has dialogue, or words that characters speak. Dialogue shows what a character thinks and feels.

 Reread to think about what makes this story realistic fiction.

 Talk about pages 128-131. Tell how you know this story is realistic fiction.

 **Write** two things you learn about the characters from the dialogue.

Check In 1 2 3 4

Characters	What the Dialogue Shows

Events can tell about problems and solutions in a story. A problem is something characters want to solve, change, or find out. The way the problem is solved is the solution.

 Reread "Now, What's That Sound?"

 Talk about Gilbert and Marta's problem. Share how they try and finally solve the problem.

Write about the problem and its solution.

Check In 1 2 3 4

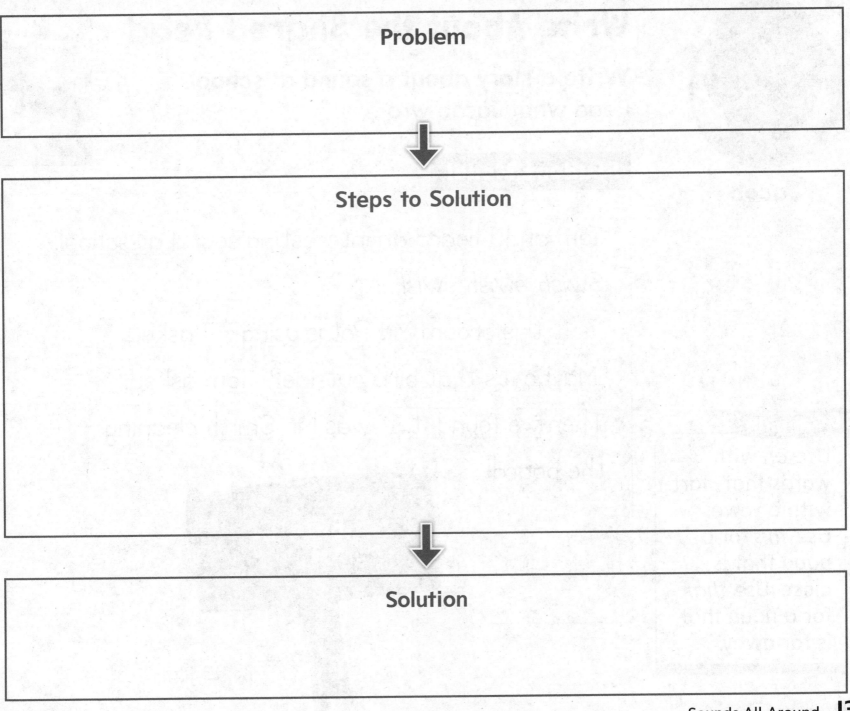

Problem

Steps to Solution

Solution

Jacob

Write About the Shared Read

Write a story about a sound at school.
Read what Jacob wrote.

Now, What's That Sound?

Student Model

Tom and I heard an interesting sound at school.

Swish, swish, swish.

"Is it this broom Mr. Pot is using?" I asked.

"Maybe it's that bird outside?" Tom asked.

Then we found it. It was Mr. Smith cleaning

the board!

Grammar

Use *an* with words that start with a vowel. Use *this* for a noun that is close. Use *that* for a noun that is far away.

Talk about details Jacob used in his writing. Underline the beginning of each sentence.

 Circle the words *an, this,* and *that.*

 Talk about why the first sentence is a good beginning to a story.

Write what you notice about Jacob's writing.

Quick Tip

You can talk about Jacob's writing using these sentence starters:

Jacob used . . .
I noticed . . .

Whistle
for
Willie
by Ezra Jack Keats

👧 **Retell** the story using the illustrations and words from the story.

✏️ **Write** about the story.

What does Peter want to do when he whistles?

_____
- -
_____
- -
_____

Text Evidence

Page

What does Peter do to feel more grown up?

_____
- -
_____
- -
_____

Text Evidence

Page

Check In   1   2   3   4

Anchor Text

 Talk about what Peter is doing on pages 231–233.

 Write clues that help you know how Peter feels when he stops.

Illustration Clues	Story Clues

How does Peter feel? How does the author let you know how Peter feels? Share your answers.

_____

- -

_____

- -

_____

- -

_____

Talk about Peter's plan on pages 234–237. Why does he want to whistle?

Write what happens on these pages.

Pages 234–235	Pages 236–237

How does the author help you know that Peter won't give up trying to whistle? Share your ideas.

_____

_____

_____

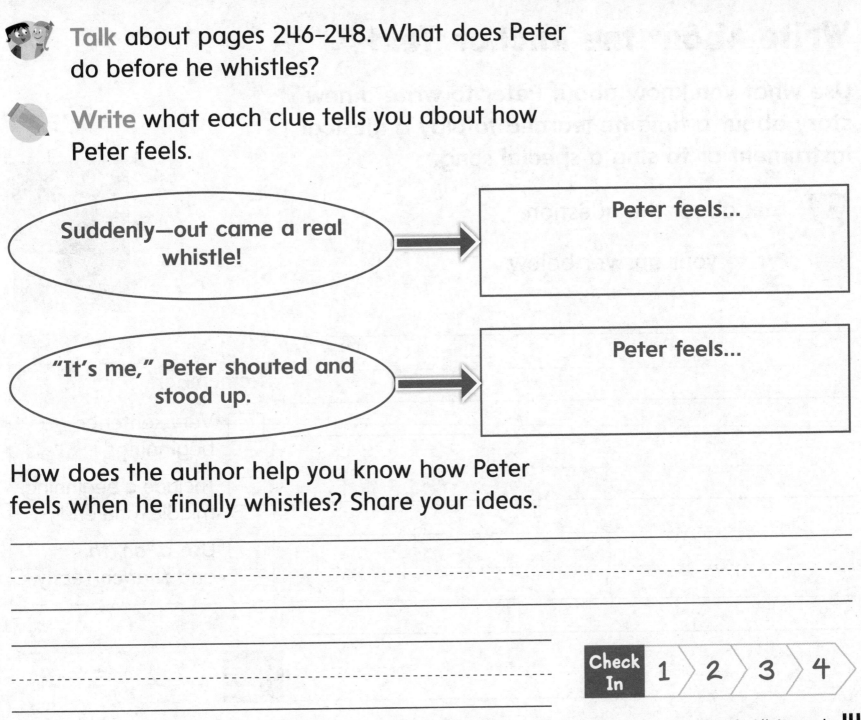

Talk about pages 246–248. What does Peter do before he whistles?

Write what each clue tells you about how Peter feels.

Suddenly—out came a real whistle! ⟶ Peter feels...

"It's me," Peter shouted and stood up. ⟶ Peter feels...

How does the author help you know how Peter feels when he finally whistles? Share your ideas.

_____

- -

_____

_____

- -

_____

Check In 1 ⟩ 2 ⟩ 3 ⟩ 4

Write About the Anchor Text

Use what you know about Peter to write a new story about a time he learned to play a musical instrument or to sing a special song.

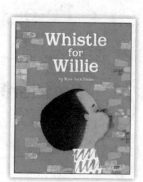

 Talk about the question.

 Write your answer below.

_____

- -

_____

- -

_____

- -

_____

Remember:

☐ Vary sentence beginnings.

☐ Include a beginning, middle, and end.

☐ Use *a*, *an*, *this*, and *that* correctly.

Check In 1 2 3 4

Shake! Strike! Strum!

Make these instruments and start a band!

How to Make a Guitar

What You Need

- tissue box
- rubber bands
- tape
- ruler

What to Do

1. Stretch four to six rubber bands around the box.

2. Tape a ruler to the back. This is the guitar's neck.

3. Decorate the guitar.

4. Strum or pluck the rubber bands.

 Read to find out how to make instruments.

Underline the first step when making a guitar.

Talk about why the author uses numbers to show the steps.

(t) Spike Mafford/Photodisc/Getty Images; (tc) Ursula Alter/Photographer's Choice RF/Getty Images; (bc) Stockdisc/PunchStock; (bl) Stockdisc/PunchStock; (b) Ken Cavanagh/McGraw-Hill Education

How to Make a Shaker

What You Need

- plastic bottle
- dried beans
- stickers

What to Do

1. Put beans into a bottle.

2. Put fun stickers on it.

3. Shake and have fun.

Now you can shake, strike, strum, and have some fun!

🔵 **Circle** the materials in the "What You Need" list that are used in step one.

🔵 **Underline** what you should do after you decorate the bottle.

🔵 **Talk** about why the author wrote three steps.

Quick Tip

Use a sentence starter to talk about the steps:

The author wrote three steps because each step . . .

Talk about the sections of the text on page 148.

 Write what each section tells about.

"What You Need"	"What to Do"

Why did the author include both sections?

_____

- -

_____

- -

_____

Write About It

Write your own how-to text. Include a list of materials and the steps to follow.

Check In 1 2 3 4

Experiment with Sounds

Step 1 **Put** a rubber band across a bowl.

Step 2 **Pull** the rubber band and let go.
Write what you see and hear.

_____

- -

_____

_____

- -

_____

_____

- -

_____

Step 3 **Pull** the rubber band again. Stop it from moving
with your hand. Talk about what you feel.

_____

- -

_____

Step 4 **Write** what you think will change if you use rubber bands and bowls of different sizes.

_____

- -

_____

- -

_____

Step 5 **Use** rubber bands and bowls of different sizes. Write the results.

_____

- -

_____

- -

_____

Step 6 **Choose** how to present your findings. You may want to give a performance using your rubber bands and bowls.

Check In 1 > 2 > 3 > 4 >

Sing the song. Then talk about what part of the car is making the last sound in the song.

 Compare the sound words with the sound words you read in "Now, What's That Sound?"

Quick Tip

Talk about the song using this sentence starter:

The sounds in the song are made by. . .

I Have a Car

I have a car, it's made of tin.
Nobody knows what shape it's in.
It has four wheels and a rumble seat.
Hear us chugging down the street.
Honk honk
Rattle rattle rattle
Crash beep beep.

Check In 1 2 3 4

Make Mystery Sounds

1 **Look** at your Build Knowledge pages in your reader's notebook. What did you learn about how sounds are made?

2 **Ask** your partner to close his or her eyes. Choose a classroom object and make a sound. Have your partner guess how you're making the sound. Take turns.

3 **Write** how your partner's sound was made. Then write how it is similar to or different from the sounds you read about in two of the texts you read this week. Use two vocabulary words from the Word Bank.

Think about what you learned this week. Fill in the bars on page 121.

Build Knowledge

Build Vocabulary

 Talk with your partner about how things get built.

 Write words about building things.

(use tools)

Building Things

Huntstock/Getty Images

My Goals

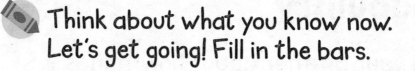

Think about what you know now. Let's get going! Fill in the bars.

What I Know Now

I can read and understand a nonfiction text.

1 > 2 > 3 > 4

I can write an opinion about a nonfiction text.

1 > 2 > 3 > 4

I know about how things get built.

1 > 2 > 3 > 4

 You will come back to the next page later.

Key
1 = I do not understand.
2 = I understand but need more practice.
3 = I understand.
4 = I understand and can teach someone.

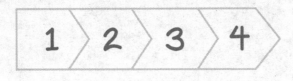 Think about what you've learned. What do you know now that you can teach others? Fill in the bars.

What I Learned

I can read and understand a nonfiction text.

1 2 3 4

I can write an opinion about a nonfiction text.

1 2 3 4

I know about how things get built.

1 2 3 4

Shared Read

 My Goal I can read and understand a nonfiction text.

 Find Text Evidence

 Read the title and look at the photo. Ask a question about something you want to learn from this text.

Talk about the ship using details in the photo.

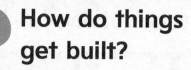 **Essential Question**

? How do things get built?

The Joy of a Ship

Nonfiction

Ships take people and things all over the world. How does a ship get made? Find out here!

Shared Read

🔍 **Find Text Evidence**

✏️ **Underline** and read aloud the words *build, above,* and *fall.*

🖍️ **Circle** and read aloud the word with the *oy* sound spelled *oy* as in *toys.*

What is needed to build a ship? Making ships employs many workers. This task uses lots of tools and parts as well. Let's see how a ship is made, step by step.

These people study the plans for the ship. There are many things to do!

Frame It!

First, workers build a frame. The ship frame can **balance** on blocks up above a dock. Huge cranes hoist the big parts in place so they do not fall. Workers must avoid being bumped by these big pieces of steel.

Some huge gantry cranes can lift 1,500 tons as high as 230 feet in the air.

Bogdan Wankowicz/Alamy Stock Photo

Sheets of Steel

🔍 **Find Text Evidence**

 Talk about details in the photos that help you understand the dangers of working with steel.

Ask a question you have about the text so far. Read to find the answer.

First, two kinds of metal are melted into steel. It boils! Hot steel flows into flat metal sheets and molds. When steel gets cold, it gets hard. The steel sheets are then ready for making a ship.

Stand back! The steel is very hot!

Digital Vision/Photodisc/Getty Images

A worker joins each steel **section** by heating the edges, called joints. Workers put on gloves and a helmet to protect their hands and head.

Find Text Evidence

Underline and read aloud the words *knew* and *money*.

Circle and read aloud each word with the sound you hear in the middle of *coin*.

Check It, Paint It

Workers check all the joints. Then they point out leaks and fix them. If a joint leaks, the inside of this ship will be moist with water. It might even sink!

Fritz Hoffmann/The Image Works

Then, the ship is painted, and this job is done! It gleams in the sun. The workers knew it would look nice! People will pay a lot of money to ride on this ship.

Shared Read

Find Text Evidence

Ask any other questions you have. Reread to find the answers.

Retell the text so it makes sense.

Out to Sea!

The people on the dock point with joy as the new ship begins the first trip! Those on the ship wave as it glides toward the open sea.

Did you know?

There are many kinds of ships on the sea.

Ice Breaker Ship ▼

Aircraft Carrier ▼

Cargo Ship ▼

Nonfiction

(tr) USCG photo by Patrick Kelley; (bl) Purestock/SuperStock; (br) Kevin Philips/Stockbyte/Getty Images

Writing Practice

Write Sentences

 Talk about the different types of ships.

Listen to this opinion about a type of ship.

> I would like to ride a ferry. They are big and have loud horns! They can take you many places.

 Underline the reasons for the opinion.

Circle the concluding statement.

Talk about what type of ship you would like to go on.

Write sentences about what type of ship you would like to go on. Give reasons for your opinion. Include a concluding statement.

_____

- -

_____

- -

_____

- -

_____

Underline the reasons for your opinion.

Circle the concluding statement.

Vocabulary

 Listen to the sentences and look at the photos.

 Talk about the words.

 **Write** your own sentences using each word.

balance

The worker can **balance** up high.

_____

- -

_____

section

This **section** is not finished yet.

_____

- -

_____

Inflectional Endings

The *-ed* ending on an action word means the action happened in the past. To figure out the meaning of a word ending in *-ed* use the meaning of the base word and the ending.

Find Text Evidence

I can use the meaning of *melt* and *-ed* to figure out that *melted* means a solid became a liquid in the past.

> First, two kinds of metal are (melted) into steel.

Your Turn

How can you figure out the meaning of *painted* on page 165? What does it mean?

_____

- -

_____

Remember, a **nonfiction** text gives facts about real things. It can include headings that give information about a section of text.

Reread "The Joy of a Ship."

Talk about the headings in the text.

Write what you learn from the headings and text on pages 161 and 166.

Heading on Page 161	Information from Heading and Text
Heading on Page 166	Information from Heading and Text

Details can give information about causes and effects in a text. A **cause** in a text is how or why something happens. An **effect** is what happens.

 Reread "The Joy of a Ship."

 Talk about the causes and effects in the text.

Write what causes hot steel to get hard. Then write about other causes and effects in the text.

Check In 1 2 3 4

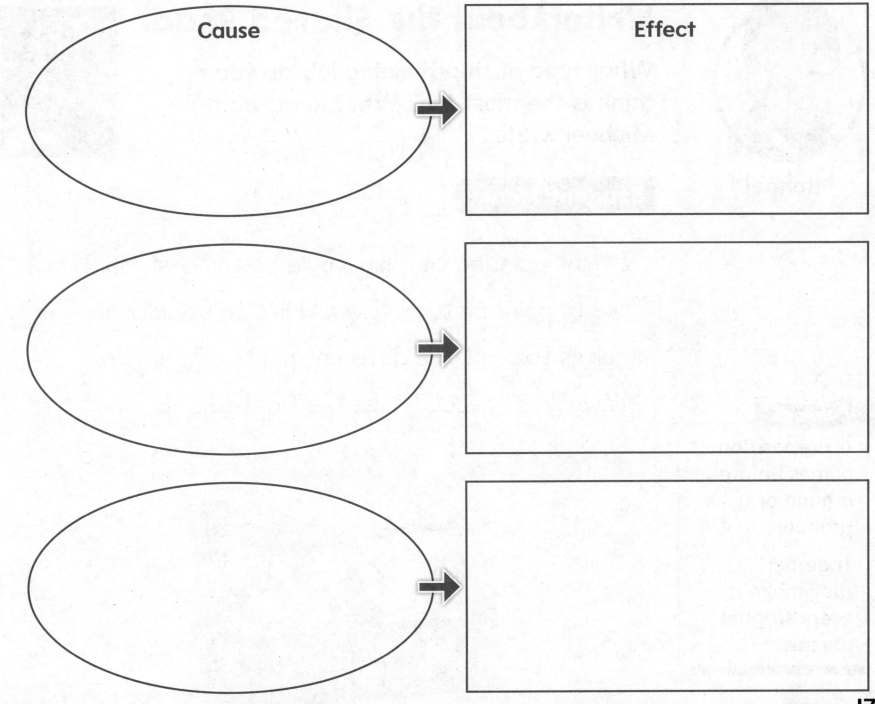

Cause

Effect

Writing and Grammar

Write About the Shared Read

What type of ship-building job do you think is the most fun? Why? Read what Michael wrote.

Michael

Student Model

I think painting the ship would be the best job. I like to paint pictures. I would like to use lots of colors to paint the different parts of the ship. It would be great to see the finished ship!

Grammar

A **preposition** comes before a noun or a pronoun.

Together they make a **prepositional phrase.**

Ivanastar/iStock/Getty Images

Talk about details Michael used. Underline the reasons for his opinion.

 Circle the prepositional phrase in the third sentence.

 Draw a box around the concluding statement.

 Write what you notice about Michael's writing.

_____

- -

_____

- -

_____

- -

_____

Building Bridges

Retell the text using the words and photos from the text.

Write about the text.

Why do some bridges have cables?

_____

- -

_____

- -

_____

Text Evidence

Page

What is the same about the arch bridge and Rolling Bridge?

_____

- -

_____

- -

_____

Text Evidence

Page

Check In | 1 | 2 | 3 | 4

Talk about the photos on pages 260–263.

Write what you read in each caption.
Talk about what the captions tell you.

Page 261	Page 262	Page 263

How does the author's use of captions help you understand the text? Share your answer.

_____

- -

_____

- -

_____

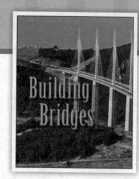

 Talk about what the author asks on pages 264–266. Where can you find the answers?

 Use clues from the questions and answers to write interesting facts about each bridge.

Firth of Forth Bridge	Golden Gate Bridge	Rolling Bridge

Why does the author ask and answer questions in the text? Share your answer.

_____

- -

_____

- -

_____

Check In 1 > 2 > 3 > 4

Write About the Anchor Text

Which bridge do you think is most interesting? Why?

Talk about the question.

Write your answer below.

Building Bridges

_____

- -

_____

- -

_____

- -

_____

- -

_____

Remember:

☐ Give reasons for your opinion.

☐ Write a concluding statement.

☐ Use prepositions correctly.

Check In 1 ⟩ 2 ⟩ 3 ⟩ 4

Small Joy

Tiny houses do not take a long time to build. Tiny houses do not cost a lot. And tiny houses do not take a lot of energy or materials. They are good for the earth!

Tiny houses can go where their owners go!

Read to find out why tiny houses are good things.

Underline three things that are good about tiny houses.

Talk about how the author feels about tiny houses.

Quick Tip

Look at punctuation marks for a clue to the author's feelings.

Dee Williams

Talk about what "joy" means.

Write clues from the text and photos that tell about tiny houses.

Clues in the Text	Clues in the Photos

Why did the author name this text "Small Joy"? Share your answer.

_____

- -

_____

- -

_____

Talk About It

How do the text, photos, and captions help you understand why people build tiny houses?

Check In 1 2 3 4

How to Build a(n) _____

Step 1 Choose something you want to learn how to build using materials found in nature.

_____
- -
_____

Step 2 Write questions about building your item.

_____
- -
_____
- -
_____
- -
_____

Step 3 Find the information you need in books or online.

Step 4 Write what you learned about how to build your item. Use a dictionary to find and spell words about the materials you can use.

Materials	Steps to Build a(n) _____

Step 5 Choose how to present your work.

Tell what you learn about the U.S. Capitol building from the photo and caption.

 Compare what you read about building a bridge to building the Capitol.

Lot 12251 (142), Library of Congress, LC-USZ6-1323

It took a lot of years, money, and people to build the U.S. Capitol building. People do important work for our government there.

Quick Tip

Compare using these sentence starters:

Building a bridge . . .

Building the Capitol also . . .

Check In 1 2 3 4

Write a Nonfiction Text

1 **Look** at your Build Knowledge pages in your reader's notebook. What did you learn about how things get built?

2 **Choose** one of the things you read about this week. Write the steps that tell how it gets built. Then compare two other things you read about. How are they built? Use two vocabulary words from the Word Bank.

3 **Draw** a picture of your building.

Think about what you learned this week. Fill in the bars on page 157.

Carla

I wrote a how-to text to teach others how to make a target game.

My Goal

I can write a how-to text.

Student Model

How to Make a Target Game

What You Need

tape that is sticky on both sides

four table tennis balls

three sheets of felt in different colors

scissors

glue

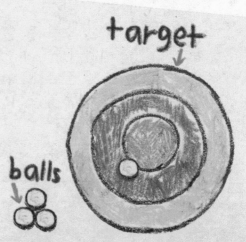

target

balls

How-To Text

My how-to text gives the steps for making something.

What to Do

1. Cover the balls with the tape.

2. Cut out three felt circles. Make a large one, a medium one, and a small one.

3. Stack and glue the felt circles from largest to smallest.

4. Hang the target on a wall. Throw a ball and watch it stick to the target!

Genre

Talk about what makes Carla's text a how-to text.

Ask any questions you have about how-to texts.

Circle the third step for how to make a target game.

Writing and Grammar

Brainstorm and Plan

 Talk about ideas for your how-to text.

Draw some of your ideas.

Quick Tip

As you brainstorm ideas, think about things you know how to do well.

How to Buckle a car seat for a little kid. How to Seat-Belt. How to take care of a little kid.
Kid me

Choose something to write a how-to text about.

How to take care of a little kid.

Describe what your how-to text will teach others to do.
Think about the steps.

My How To text will teach peap to how to take care of a little kid.

Draft

Read Carla's draft of her how-to text.

Focus on a Topic

I focused on one topic in my how-to text.

Student Model

How to Make a Target Game

What You Need

tape that is sticky on both sides

four table tennis balls

felt in different colors

scissors

glue

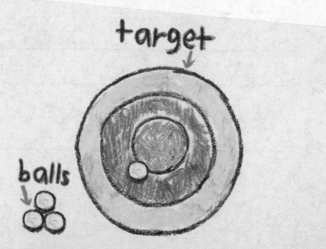

target

balls

Sentence Fluency

I made some sentences long and some sentences short.

What to Do

1. Cover the balls with the tape.

2. Cut out three felt circles.

3. Stack and glue the felt circles from largest to smallest.

4. Hang the target.

Steps in a Process

The steps in my how-to text are in order.

Your Turn

Begin to write your how-to text in your writer's notebook. Use your ideas from pages 190–191. Make sure you focus on your topic. Tell your steps in order.

Check In 1 2 3 4

Writing and Grammar

Revise and Edit

Think about how Carla revised and edited her how-to text.

I added details to give more information.

Student Model

How to Make a Target Game

What You Need

tape that is sticky on both sides

I used the Word Bank to spell words correctly.

four table tennis balls

three sheets of felt in different colors

scissors

glue

target

balls

I added a preposition to tell where to hang the target.

Specific Words

I used specific words in my how-to text.

Grammar

- A preposition is a word that comes before a noun. Some prepositions are: *in, on* and *above.*

What to Do

1. Cover the balls with the tape.

2. Cut out three felt circles. Make a large one, a medium one, and a small one.

3. Stack and glue the felt circles from largest to smallest.

4. Hang the target on a wall. Throw a ball and watch it stick to the target!

Concluding Statement

I added information to make my ending interesting.

Your Turn

Revise and edit your writing. Use prepositions correctly. Include a concluding statement.

Check In   1   2   3   4

Publish and Present

 Finish editing your writing. Make sure it is neat and ready to publish.

 Practice presenting your work with a partner. Use this checklist.

 Present your work.

Review Your Work	Yes	No
Speaking and Listening		
I paid attention to the tone of my piece.	☐	☐
I spoke loudly and clearly.	☐	☐
I asked questions if I didn't understand something.	☐	☐

Talk with a partner about what you did well in your writing.

Write about your work.

 What did you do well in your writing?

_____

_____

_____

What do you need to work on?

_____

_____

_____

 Think about your goal of writing a how-to text.

Check In | 1 | 2 | 3 | 4

Connect to Science

Find Text Evidence

Ask yourself questions about the story. Read to find the answers.

Circle the things Penny and Mom see in the night sky.

Talk about what makes the night sky special.

The Night Sky

"Wow!" said Penny.

"What are you reading?" asked Mom.

Penny put her book down. "There are billions of stars in the sky!" she said. "Can we stay up late to see them?"

"Sure," said Mom.

Later, Penny watched out the window and waited for the stars. But the couch was comfy. And she was sleepy. Soon, she was fast asleep.

The next night, Mom set up a tent outside. They watched the Sun set, and the sky turned pink and purple. Suddenly, it got very dark. Bright specks of light scattered all across the sky.

Penny squealed, "There are so many stars!" She could watch them twinkle all night. But her sleeping bag was comfy. And she was sleepy. Soon, she was fast asleep.

Connect to Science

🔍 Find Text Evidence

 Ask yourself questions about the text. Read to find the answers.

 Circle why stars are important.

Talk about the different shapes stars make in the sky.

Billions of Stars

Look up at the night sky. What do you see? There are billions of stars scattered across the sky, more than anyone can count!

A star is made of burning gas. This makes the star glow with bright light.

There is one star we see every day: our Sun! Other stars may look tiny, but some are the same size as our Sun. They are just very far away.

A solar system is a group of planets. Stars, like our Sun, are important to solar systems. They give light and warmth.

A group of stars is called a constellation. People give names to constellations based on the shapes stars make in the sky.

On a clear night, try to find a constellation. Or make up your own with the shapes you see in the night sky!

Talk about the constellation in the photo.

Take Notes

SCIENCE

Connect to Science

Compare the Passages

 Talk about what you learn about the sky from "The Night Sky" and "Billions of Stars."

 Compare and contrast what you learn about the sky from each text.

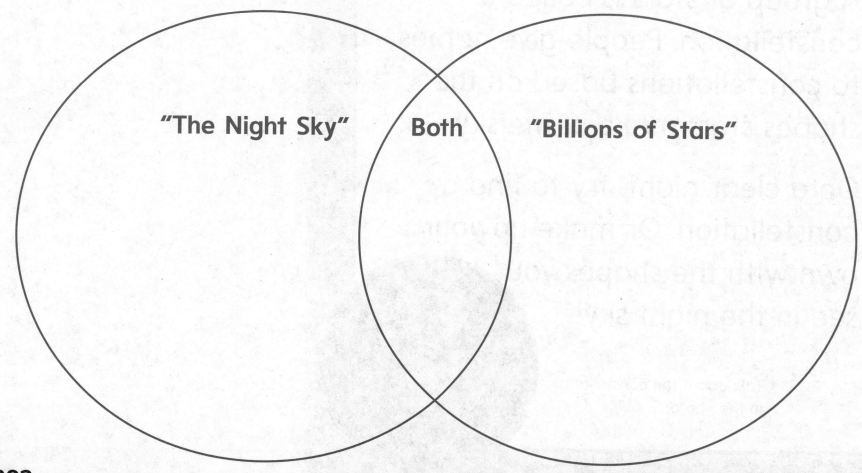

"The Night Sky"   Both   "Billions of Stars"

Write what you learned about the sky from each text.

_____
- -
_____
- -
_____
- -
_____
- -
_____
- -
_____

Connect to Science

Observe the Sky

 Talk about what we see in the sky during the day. Talk about what we see at night.

What to do

1. **Observe** the sky during the day. Do not look

   directly at the Sun. Draw what you see.

2. **Observe** the sky at night. Draw what you see.

3. **Compare** your data. Do you see the same

   things in the day and night sky?

4. **Write** what you observed.

You need

pencil

crayons

What you observe

My observations

Extend Your Learning

Choose Your Own Book

Minutes I Read

 Tell a partner about a book you want to read. Say why you want to read it.

Write the title.

_____

- -

_____

Write about your opinion of the book you read. Give reasons for your opinion.

_____

- -

_____

- -

_____

- -

_____

Think About Your Learning

 Think about what you learned this unit.

 Write one thing you did well.

_____

- -

_____

- -

_____

 Write one thing that you want to get better at.

_____

- -

_____

- -

_____

Share a goal you have with a partner.

My Sound-Spellings

Aa apple — a

Bb bat — b

Cc camel — c ck k

Dd dolphin — d _ed

Ee egg — e ea

Ff fire — f ph

Gg guitar — g

Hh hippo — h_

Ii insect — i

Jj jump — j dge ge gi_

Kk koala — c k ck

Ll lemon — l _le

Mm map — m

Nn nest — n kn_ gn

Oo octopus — o

Pp piano — p

Qq queen — qu_

Rr rose — r wr_

Ss sun — s ce ci_

Tt turtle — t _ed

Uu umbrella — u

Vv volcano — v

Ww window — w_

Xx box — x

Yy yo-yo — y_

Zz zipper — z _s

th thumb	sh shell	ch tch cheese	wh_ whale	ng sing	a ai_ _ay a_e ea ei train	i y i_e igh ie five
o oa ow o_e _oe boat	u u_e _ew _ue cube	e_e ea ee e _y ie _ey tree	ar star	er ir ur or shirt	oar or ore corn	ow ou cow
oi _oy boy	oo book	oo u_e u _ew ue ou ui spoon	a aw au augh al straw	air are ear ere chair		

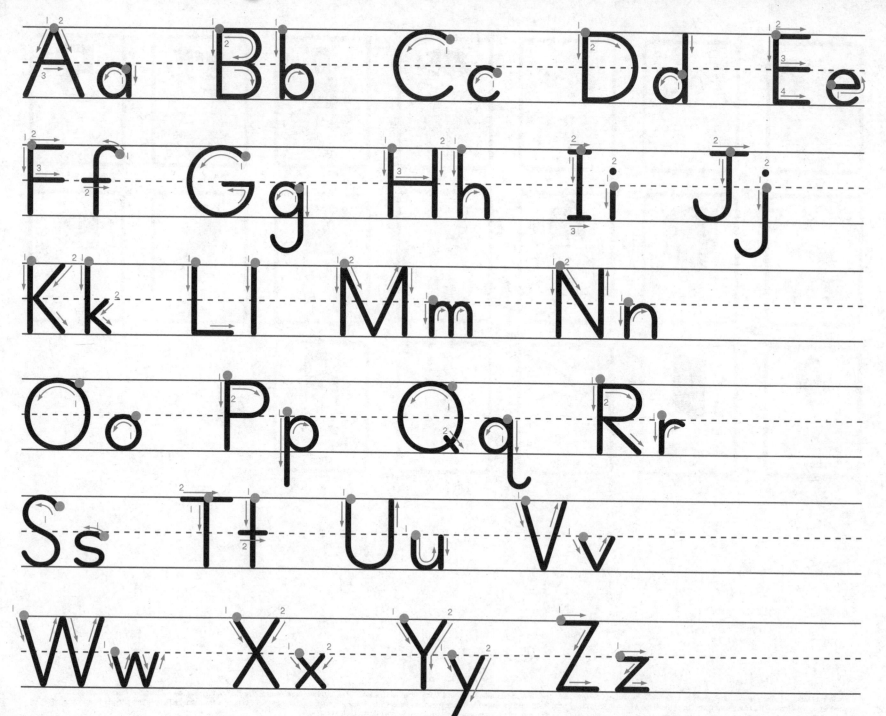